A Matter of Selection

poems by

Carol Smallwood

Poetic Matrix Press

Front Cover Art by Vera Gubnitskaia
http://vera-gubnitskaia-art.blogspot.com

Poetic Matrix Press
www.poeticmatrix.com

A Matter of Selection

Acknowledgments

Catching On: *Divining the Prime Meridian* (WordTech Editions, 2015)

A Chemo Visit: *Water, Earth, Air, Fire, and Picket Fences* (Lamar University Press, 2014)

Galaxies: *Prisms, Particles, and Refractions* (Finishing Line Press, 2017)

Grade School Dream: *Compartments: Poems on Nature, Femininity and Other Realms* (Anaphora Literary Press, 2011)

I Divine: *Compartments: Poems on Nature, Femininity and Other Realms* (Anaphora Literary Press, 2011)

Icons: *Prisms, Particles, and Refractions* (Finishing Line Press, 2017)

It is Hard to Accept: *In Hubble's Shadow* (Shanti Arts, 2017)

The Last Doll: *Water, Earth, Air, Fire, and Picket Fences* (Lamar University Press, 2014)

A Matter of Lines: *Water, Earth, Air, Fire, and Picket Fences* (Lamar University Press, 2014)

On the Way: *Parentheses Journal* March, 2017

Patterns: *In Hubble's Shadow* (Shanti Arts, 2017)

Photographs: *In Hubble's Shadow* (Shanti Arts, 2017)

Probate: *English Journal,* January, 2006; *Divining the Prime Meridian* (WordTech Editions, 2015)

Prufrock Napkins: *Water, Earth, Air, Fire, and Picket Fences* (Lamar University Press, 2014)

The Radio Said: *Divining the Prime Meridian* (WordTech Editions, 2015)

The Sewing Box: *Compartments: Poems on Nature, Femininity and Other Realms* (Anaphora Literary Press, 2011)

Sewing by Day: *Parentheses Journal* March, 2017

Shopping at Tom's: *Compartments: Poems on Nature, Femininity and Other Realms* (Anaphora Literary Press, 2011)

Sleeping Beauty: *A Successful Completion* (Diversion Press, 2017)

There Were Only: *Prisms, Particles, and Refractions* (Finishing Line Press, 2017)

A Tree: *Parentheses Journal* March, 2017

Water Puddles: *Prisms, Particles, and Refractions* (Finishing Line Press, 2017)

We Select: *The Binnacle: Thirteenth Annual International Ultra-Short Competition Edition*, University of Maine at Machias, 2016; *In the Measuring* (Shanti Arts, 2017)

Wind in Trees: *In Hubble's Shadow,* (Shanti Arts, 2017)

Year After Year: *Divining the Prime Meridian* (WordTech Editions, 2015)

You Know: *Prisms, Particles, and Refractions* (Finishing Line Press, 2017)

Foreword

I've worked with countless writers since starting *The Bookends Review* in 2012, yet I've rarely—if ever—come across someone whose poetic abilities—in terms of both structural explorations and thematic variety—match their levels of academic exploration and altruistic warmth. Carol Smallwood is one such multifaceted spirit, as she ceaselessly investigates both the technical plateaus of the genre and the motivations, inspirations, and successes of those who produce within it. (See her continual series of interviews on our site for proof.)

Of course, her greatest strengths lie in her own original content, and in that respect, *A Matter of Selection* soars not only as a follow-up to her past collections, but also as an independent entry into the modern poetic landscape. Be it the personal touches inside the profound "The Universe," the sensory allusions of "A Chemo Visit," the domestic snapshots shaping "The Sewing Box," or the startling social commentary beneath the short and simple "Examples," Smallwood ensures that just about every piece is surprising, unique, and resonant. As such, *A Matter of Selection* is a tour-de-force illustration of the potentials of poetry.

—Jordan Blum, founder, editor-in-chief, *The Bookends Review*

Contents

A Matter of Selection

Prologue

I.
Nature

IV
Speculations

Epilogue

A Matter of Selection

Preface

We continuously select, make choices, some good, some bad—the full outcome we won't know until after we'd made them; and the word selection is tied to Darwin's theory of natural selection we're still struggling with—those best adapted to their environment have the tendency to survive. After Darwin, came Freud who delved into the selection complexities of our conscious and subconscious—still in the frontier of science.

The more I write, the more what Octavio Paz observed comes to mind: "Poetry is not what words say but what is said between them, that which appears fleetingly in pauses and silences." When I read the work of others, it's the whispered that has the most impact.

The seventy-one poems are a mix of free verse and formal poetry grouped into: Part I Nature; Part II Moments in Time; Part III The Domestic; Part IV Speculations. It is hoped readers will enjoy them as much as I had writing them.

My sincere thank goes to Jordan Blum, founder and editor-in-chief, *The Bookends Review* for the foreword; to blurb writers: Evan Mantyk, president, The Society of Classical Poets; Cristina Deptula, executive editor, *Synchronized Chaos Magazine*, Mary Barnet, founder & editor-in-chief, PoetryMagazine.com; Rebecca Resinski, editorial board, *Heron Tree*, professor of Classics, Hendrix College; Julie Damerell, editor, *Miller's Pond*.

Prologue

We Select

a few—the selections random: a melody, morning fog, a path,
knowing with certainty at the time they'll be ours to the end—
an imprinting sudden as first love with no thought of aftermath:
a sunset, muffled cry, a Thanksgiving dressing, smile of a friend.

Knowing with certainty at the time they'll be ours to the end,
they return at unexpected moments, their clarity a surprise:
a sunset, muffled cry, a Thanksgiving dressing, smile of a friend
bringing feeling from depths we cannot withhold, disguise.

They return at unexpected moments, their clarity a surprise
an imprinting sudden as first love with no thought of aftermath
bringing feeling from depths we cannot withhold, disguise:
a few—the selections random: a melody, morning fog, a path.

I.
Nature

The Universe

It must be true: the Universe has no edge or center as I've read
so it brings me security to make patchwork quilts at night;
it makes sense to cut up pieces to sew with needle and thread.

"You are not lonely when you sew," Grandmother often said
as she sewed apron after apron with evident delight;
It must be true: the Universe has no edge or center as I've read.

Other activities most likely should have been my stead:
quilt after quilt I've made at night sitting straight, upright:
it makes sense to cut up pieces to sew with needle and thread.

Mixing pattern with plain, varying width until ready for bed,
securing the needle easy to spot on a piece extra bright—
it must be true: the Universe has no edge or center as I've read.

Fleece, flannel, denim, have made many a patchwork spread
and those who receive them do express thanks forthright:
it makes sense to cut up squares to sew with needle and thread.

I've concluded I'll have no edge or center when I'm dead
and finding security sewing squares is better than fright.
It must be true: the Universe has no edge or center as I've read
it makes sense to cut up pieces to sew with needle and thread.

Year After Year

they appear, mounds on my lawn—
newly dug soil more noticeable
in snow.

Year after year new pyramids
come with the suddenness of dreams,
the persistence of pharaohs
for immortality.

You may suggest reading about moles,
(the burrows too small for gophers)
but each year brings more fear for
all things subterranean.

The Water Cycle Selects

The water that falls on your umbrella has a good chance of having been around
since the planet cooled—a seasoned traveler of sky and ground in many places
appearing as ice, fog, rain, snow, clouds, and oceans cover 73% of our ground.

How the drops of rain selects your umbrella depends when clouds breakdown
which would require a long study of the rain's travel from its innumerable bases:
the water that falls on your umbrella has a good chance of having been around.

Most of the water on the earth's surface evaporates, then it condenses down
and it comes to earth again and if the time is right may select our workplaces,
appearing as ice, fog, rain, snow, clouds, and oceans cover 73% of our ground.

If you live in the Artic Circle, your weather couldn't help having snow abound
but if your home was near the Equator, snow won't be predicted on databases:
the water that falls on your umbrella has a good chance of having been around.

Precipitation, part of the water cycle as sleet or hail is often seen to come down
when the temperature gets low enough and precipitation forms in many cases
appearing as ice, fog, rain, snow, clouds, and oceans cover 73% of our ground.

Rain falling on umbrellas whether large or small makes a soothing sound
when walking for exercise or just being out on the town—it refreshes our faces:
the water that falls on your umbrella has a good chance of having been around
appearing as ice, fog, rain, snow, clouds, and oceans cover 73% of our ground.

Wind in Trees

is a tale that comes and goes:
like the famous oracles of Delphi
the story lies with the interpreter.

The Passing Fields

There are fields I drive by every day with the greenest weeds—not many—
a sprinkling early spring between the crops growing precisely rows in
newly plowed ground. The weeds, a lush green, lord over the brown fields
until the corn, sugar beets, or wheat grows—some of the weeds hugging
the ground, others miniature Eiffel Towers.

Every spring I wonder where they come from and conclude most seeds
are carried by the wind or were already in the ground last fall. Among the
regular rows of crops that grow in exact distance from one another, weeds
appear as if a bravado, victory over the odds—and they expected to be
even more lush when crops turned dull gold and they were still reveling
in their luck of not being between sidewalk cracks, lording over the
groundling crops like gothic spires.

I wonder what they're called and when they began—for sure millions of
years older than the crop strains. Maybe it is the chance placement of the
weeds on plowed fields that gives pause—the randomness and also the
knowing if the fields were not plowed each spring, trees, shrubs, grass,
and other vegetation would take over and return it to what it was for
millions of years before humans graduated from hunters and gatherers.

Farmers and gardeners look at weeds differently of course—weeds that
whether it rains or not grow faster than what has cost them time and
money to plant. Still, I cannot help but smile at their ability annually to
beat even those spring harbingers, the dandelions.

Water Puddles

reflect skies with such
clarity I'm a child again,
staring at trees upside
down till tipsy—
not remembering
underfoot lava flows
rivaling the heat
of the Sun.

The Naming

Who would imagine names the Purslane family of weeds would include
Common Burdock, Horsenettle, Field Pennycress, and many more;
Wild Carrot more widely known as Queen Anne's Lace is in the brood.

Some young leaves like the Dandelion (lion's tooth) are a health food
and English Daisy, Milkweed can be found mentioned in popular lore:
who would imagine names the Purslane family of weeds would include?

The family also includes Poison Ivy creating its own kind of mood—
getting too close to this one may end up with a trip to the drugstore.
Wild Carrot more widely known as Queen Anne's Lace is in the brood.

Wild Strawberry, Nimblewill, Orange Hawkweed aren't what you'd
expect and Redroot Pigweed, Purple Deadnettle, are more to look for:
who would imagine names the Purslane family of weeds would include?

Silvery Thread Moss, Creeping Speedwell, Chickory, one can conclude
would be fun to identify—Prostrate Pigweed would be hard to ignore:
Wild Carrot more widely known as Queen Anne's Lace is in the brood.

It would have been great to have a chance to name one when viewed
walking on a summer day in a field, deep woods, or open rolling moor;
who would imagine names the Purslane family of weeds would include?
Wild Carrot more widely known as Queen Anne's Lace is in the brood.

Plants

by the roadsides, ditches, railroad tracks
are among the last of their species:
in plain sight invisible.

A Tree

It stands out from others no matter the season—
a skeleton tall, frail, pale, without leaves or bark;
why it's that way I wonder, try and guess the reason.
When it rains or snows it looks even more stark.

A skeleton tall, frail, pale, without leaves or bark
stretching upwards by a road less traveled by night,
when it rains or snows it looks even more stark,
ghostlike as if doomed by some fatal decay or blight.

Stretching upwards by a road less traveled by night
why it's that way I wonder, try and guess the reason—
ghostlike as if doomed by some fatal decay or blight
it stands out from others no matter the season.

Galaxies

Just a hundred years ago we thought the Milky Way
the only one. We know little about the dark matter
holding galaxies together or dark energy pushing
them apart: but we do know when two collide—
one survives.

Dog Days Triptych

Ever wonder what the Dog Days of Summer are about?
The ancient Greeks needed to explain illness, storms,
fever, high temperature, war, disasters like drought.
Ever wonder what the Dog Days of Summer are about?
They are named for (Sirius) Dog Star, brightest no doubt
in the Canis Major constellation—bright out of the norm.
Ever wonder what the Dog Days of Summer are about?
The ancient Greeks needed to explain illness, storms.

I thought they were when dogs slept because it was so hot
and read it was translated into English about 500 years ago
covering July 3 to August 11, dates I was never taught:
I thought they were when dogs slept because it was so hot.
Grandmother often said, "Shake the yellow dog" I thought
to make one get rid of being lazy, stop going with the flow.
I thought dog days were dogs sleeping because it was so hot
and read it was translated into English about 500 years ago.

The constellation appears in Homer's, *The Iliad,* as the star
brightest at night being connected with suffering, disaster
named Orion's Dog: an evil visible point in the sky afar.
The constellation appears in Homer's, *The Iliad,* as the star
Sirius raising late in the dark liquid sky—a tale without par,
a classic for years and years of many a good schoolmaster.
The constellation appears in Homer's, *The Iliad,* as the star
brightest at night being connected with suffering, disaster.

Constellation Tercets

Orion

Orion, the mythical hunter with his companion bow
  said to be an easy constellation to spot in night sky
    is mentioned in Virgil, Homer, and the Bible.

That Orion's brightest stars, Rigel and Betelgeuse,
  and the two others said to make them is to defy
    vision and requires much speculation.

But it could be a Rorschach—each of us interprets
  what we view—a long accepted cut and dry
    concept why there's so many constellations.

Leo

The constellation, Leo, said to look like a lion that in
  Greek myth had fur that couldn't be pierced, claws
    sharper than any sword.

The outline made of Leo seen in many books looks more
  like a tea kettle or an iron to me—giving pause
    it was a man who named it.

Tradition says the huge lion was killed by Hercules as part
  of his twelve labors which makes sense because
    I've never seen a lion in the sky.

On the Way

from town today there was a square large field, all white
dazzling under a late summer sky with Queen Anne's Lace:
near Gary's Funeral Home, lace flooded the field with light—
the celebration of such delicate abandon seemed out of place.

Dazzling under a late summer sky with Queen Anne's Lace
after the new addition to the County Commission on Aging
the celebration of such delicate abandon seemed out of place:
under lofty rolling cumulus August clouds a brash staging.

After the new addition to the County Commission on Aging
edged by a rim, a gray cemetery of felled trees by the woods,
under lofty rolling cumulus August clouds a brash staging:
an unexpected stranger on the outskirts of the neighborhood.

Edged by a rim, a gray cemetery of felled trees by the woods
near Gary's Funeral Home lace flooded the field with light—
an unexpected stranger on the outskirts of the neighborhood:
from town today there was a square large field, all white.

Dirt Roads

Dirt roads as reality checks are to be recommended:
sans grass, cement, asphalt, tar, they reveal
naturalness, a useful reflection to be commended—
the passage of seasons, time, what is real.

Sans grass, cement, asphalt, tar, they reveal
footprints, tire tracks, proof of what's been,
the passage of seasons, time, what is real
so plainly to make you dare glimpse within.

Footprints, tire tracks, proof of what's been
between plants nearly extinct growing by the road
so plainly to make you dare glimpse within
as the plants only grow there wild, unbowed.

Between plants nearly extinct growing by the road
the road sees rain, ice, snow come and go
as the plants only grow there wild, unbowed
while punctuated here and there with a crow.

The road sees rain, ice, snow come and go
holes keep appearing no matter how often graded
while punctuated here and there with a crow:
leafy arms of maple and elm make them shaded.

Holes keep appearing no matter how often graded,
a sure incentive for cars to slow down,
leafy arms of maple and elm make them shaded
while drivers bounce with increasing frowns.

A sure incentive for cars to slow down:
naturalness, a useful reflection to be commended—
while drivers bounce with increasing frowns;
Dirt roads as reality checks are to be recommended.

Photographs

of Earth reveal a
naked blue marble
with cloud wisps.

I make Florida orange,
Japan purple like my
childhood globe secured
by longitude and latitude.

Thoughts on Light

In oceans too deep for light,
species generate bioluminescence;
it's also useful out of water—
fireflies use it to locate mates.

The first Australians made pictures
from spaces formed by darkness
where there were no stars.

The first mirrors must've been
bodies of water, faces,
surfaces that reflect.

What do we mean when we say the
word, light? It all depends:
my dictionary has 53 definitions.

Choice of Navigators

Polaris holds such important because the Earth's axis points at the star
Almost directly and it is also called the Pole Star, Lodestar, Cynosure,
And North Star. Chosen by navigators since early times since it's by far
The most constant in the same northern horizon position, a point secure
All year which can't be said for brighter stars. In *Julius Caesar* we read
"I am as constant as the northern star" and in Shakespeare's other work
The guiding star is used as a symbol of constancy. You'll not be mislead
If I share that Spenser described it as a "steadfast star" and it still lurks
In the writing of modern writers. Polaris holds constant while the whole
Northern sky moves around it and can be trusted more than one of our
Compasses subject to magnetic variations. Another finding we can extol
Is it's getting brighter which isn't explained by those in scientific power.
On the Alaskan Flag appears gold stars forming the familiar constellation
The Big Dipper and North Star for the most northern state in the nation.

The Big Corn Field

The big corn field was gone today:
A machine crouched amid the fray
Like a locust after a feast
Near the side road facing southeast—
Likely to be gone by Sunday.

The corn had turned from day to day
Yellow-green to deep green array
Then the pallor of baker's yeast...
The big corn field.

The next step: to plow all away
And let the shorn stubble decay
Then the field would appear deceased
All—from north to south, west to east
Nothing left behind to convey
The big corn field.

II.
Moments in Time

My Earliest Memory

is trying to catch something—
it moved on the wall of the
house when I walked in a
jacket with many buttons.

In college while covering
Plato's Cave the memory
of it resurfaced and that
it was my shadow.

Septet

I
Routine, the everyday, is what we flee
but it allows us to see strangeness in the
ordinary, wide variances in one color

The hum-drum lets us hear the distant
drummer—and see just one in a crowd
of daffodils

II
Snow tells of passing cars, who
came up the walk, deer tracks,
the prevailing wind

Save yourself backaches, paying
for shoveling: snow covers
what's come before

III
Limitations of logical atomism,
critique of understanding,
ascribability argument

Entering philosophy class,
I know Room 207 is Room 207—
exiting I'm not sure

IV
I went to the old part of the
cemetery. Leaves whirlpooled
crumbled names I could not read

Why did you die at 23, leaving
my mother without a mother—
a grave passed on to me?

V
As a child, love is as self-evident as
proclamations in grade school of the
Declaration of Independence

As teenagers, love merges with
sex making it not so self-evident

VI
Snow swirled across the highway
like sand on the Sahara; I heard
The Hanging Gardens of Babylon
succumbed to sand

VII
We shed all our skin every seven years,
distributing ourselves a few cells at
a time

It's good we're not snakes—
imagine all those human skins

Stamps

1 cent kestrels
2 cent woodpeckers
3 cent bluebirds
10's with Salvador Dali clocks
  before they melted
23's with a green George Washington
  (from crossing the Delaware?)

When I used my 33's and 34's
the clerk said (with a smile)
37 should remain a while
Then came 39's, 41's

Stamps perform marvelous feats
Superman was 32 not long ago

Safety of Predictability

A lack of sleep encourages awareness in the safety of predictability:
you think of clocks, the rhythm of day and night—that total quiet is rare.
Sleeplessness encourages losing civility, a definite increase in irritability,
a fear others know what you're thinking and will banish you elsewhere.

You think of clocks, the rhythm of day and night—that total quiet is rare.
There's fear of the unknown, an uneasiness gravity will come to an end
a fear others know what you're thinking and will banish you elsewhere
and you fight the sinking feeling it could be the end—useless to pretend.

There's fear of the unknown, an uneasiness gravity will come to an end;
sleeplessness encourages losing civility, a definite increase in irritability
and you fight the sinking feeling it could be the end—useless to pretend.
A lack of sleep encourages awareness in the safety of predictability.

Form

Growing up I put metal curlers on my fingers
    to keep them slim, held my breath for a
    smaller waist, peered in mirrors in hopes
    of seeing magazine models.

When married, I basked in the glow of my
    husband's image in Jackie Kennedy
    white gloves and when he no longer looked,
    turned to tie-dye and madras.

Then I was in a bedroom alone that echoed,
    a beveled mirror repeating my reflection
    endlessly till telescoping in another behind.

When children began dating, I attributed the
    new lines on my face to the sun saying
    there was time enough yet left.

Then gray hair obscured as clouds used in
    Greek drama; I stand in store aisles to
    prove I have form.

A Chemo Visit

In the chemo room it's impossible
to tell if the doors are opening or
closing in a hall that did not echo.

The big wrinkled chairs were elephant
tan; yellow containers shouted,
Biohazard Warning.

A woman entered and swallowed by
an elephant chair stared at the TV,
till shouting, "None of them say
they're the father of her baby."

A dozing man with Christopher Reeves
profile flung his hands as if flying
and woke with a crooked cap.

Perhaps it is better not to listen to
doors in a hall that did not echo.

Probate

Personal Property:
One working team
" driving horse, named Jack
" black cow
" black heifer, 2 years old
" grain binder, no twine
" grain drill
" walking plow
" harrow
" wagon, one spare wheel
" buggy, newly painted red

To my son, Jim, I give, devise and bequeath, the sum of One Dollar.

To my daughter, Mary, I give, devise and bequeath, the sum of
One Dollar.

All the rest, residue and remainder of my estate, real, personal and
mixed, wheresoever situate, I give, devise and bequeath unto and to
the use of my wife, Sarah.

(A letter from Mary: I am returning the One Dollar.)

Acoustic Ceilings and Tile Floors

Doctor visits are laying on tables looking at ceiling tiles,
looking down on tile floors while weighed on scales
all the time thinking you'd like to be visiting the British Isles,
picturing extravagant meals in the garden of Versailles.

Looking down on tile floors while weighed on scales
you count the white flecks in one of the beige squares
picturing extravagant meals in the garden of Versailles
and what life must be like for a charge d'affaires.

You count the white flecks in one of the beige squares;
do you have time to count them all—
and what life must be like for a charge d'affaires
to not wonder what made a dent in the white wall.

Do you have time to count them all
while not looking at the long scissors on tables?
To not wonder what made a dent in the white wall
you try to guess how many others thought of fables.

While not looking at the long scissors on tables
waiting for the doctor to walk through the door
you try to guess how many others thought of fables
any other thing to take you away, make you soar

waiting for the doctor to walk through the door.
All the time thinking you'd like to be visiting the British Isles,
any other thing to take you away, make you soar.
Doctor visits are laying on tables looking at ceiling tiles.

It is Hard to Accept

White is really all colors,
blood appears blue in veins

That matter can be solid,
liquid, or gas—and when
temperature is high enough
molecules fly apart

That child and wife abuse
thrives under the cover
of religion

But biology explains:
we really see upside down

Grade School Dream

A bunch of us girls at St. John's
were washing our hands at recess
and suddenly Sally knifed Ruth in
the back and red curled down
white blouses as the rest joined in.

Then, without a word we washed,
walked up the stairs with bowed
heads to catechism class to study
which sins were venial and which
were mortal.

Two-Faced Janus

The worship of Janus goes back to Romulus even before the start
of the city of Rome as the god of beginnings, gates, transitions, time,
duality, doorways, passages, and endings. Janus presided over the part
of ending of conflict and war and peace—his temple doors open anytime
in time of war, were closed to mark the peace. As a god of transitions,
he had many temples erected to him and was connected with activities
pertaining to birth, journeys and exchanges, and associated with missions
with Portunus, a harbor god, concerned with traveling safety agility.
It is agreed that the first month of the year, January, is for Janus acclaimed
for having two opposite faces, the ability to see all things in past phase
and future. Around 450 BCE, January became the first 30 days reclaimed
on the Roman calendar; later Julius Caesar added a day to make it 31 days.
Janus remains a solid example of the middle ground—between barbarity
and civilization, youth and adulthood, urban cities and insularity.

I Divine

women poets in anthologies,
my fingers forked sticks probing
what lies underneath.

But the few found can but
use the language of men—
I leave thirsty.

Dreams of Flying

"You know, when I come back to River City, I turn
into what I once was," said Karen. I hadn't seen her
since our last school reunion and her eyes looked
blurred—it could be contacts. I'd stayed in
River City known for the world's largest man-made
sand pile from dredging in lumbering days,

which sat like a pyramid on the Nile; on days
of high wind when it wasn't wet or weather had a turn
of snow, it made eyes smart. Perhaps a man-made
answer explained Karen's blurred look. She waved her
hand with many rings saying her husband had left in
a hurry with a woman who sold tennis balls, then looked

out the window saying, "I loved him but looked
like I didn't like him and I've spent so many long days
crying," then showed me pictures of her poodles. In
time the talk was about classmates, and in turn
I asked if she liked the service. She'd done well, her
rise was rapid and she'd been able to buy man-made

goods I could never have. Twisting a man-made
heart shaped ring she waited a minute, and then looked
at me to ask, "What's your idea of Heaven?, her
tone returning to the best friend of high school days.
She continued, "I've been having these dreams. I turn
and twist among dark blue clouds looking down in

flight seeing days go by, listening, everything in
plain sight, not afraid of falling or landing in man-made
or natural places and easily fly, effortlessly turn
to gulp fresh air, satisfying a deep thirst it looked
I never had. When I awake I feel cast out for days."
We talked about River City and I poured her

more coffee and after salad the talk changed to her
aunt she was visiting. I just couldn't forget that in
high school she dropped me, joined the in crowd only days
into our junior year. My husband had left no man-made
things when he left in a hurry: hard as I tried it looked
like I had little to give her than lunch in turn.

Not many days after I heard Karen was dead. I saw her
turn and say, "looked like I didn't like him" recalled
her list of man-made things, dropping me in high school.

In the Civil War

Acoustic shadows occurred when sound failed to travel
due to wind currents, buildings, and obstructions
making soldiers think their mind must've unraveled
because what else could be their deductions?

Due to wind currents, buildings, and obstructions
soldiers smelled smoke, saw light from battle
because what else could be their deductions
since sound didn't reach them in the saddle.

Soldiers could smell smoke, saw light from battle
making soldiers think their mind must've unraveled
since sound didn't reach them in the saddle.
Acoustic shadows occurred when sound failed to travel.

Icons

After watching a program on the Sphinx,
my cat with outstretched paws seemed
to copy its mystery.

Theories abound about the Sphinx—
as many questions as the *Mona Lisa*.

The more icons are studied in plain sight
the less (like cats) we know of them.

Answers I'd Like to Know

If Lucifer had a wife

Why snow's white

Why clerks say how much
we've saved when paying

What language the
multi-lingual dream

If tigers really have
striped skin

Why we know more of
the surface of the
Moon than ourselves

What Does it Mean?

"It is what it is" a clerk replied to my comment how busy she was last week.
Has it any meaning—could it be profound wisdom—or just another cliché?
There's something about the saying that's mysterious, illusive, unique—
is it a passing figure of speech soon dated, already has had its heyday?

Has it any meaning—could it be profound wisdom—or just another cliché?
Maybe what it means depends on a shrug, raised eyebrow, tone, or frown.
Is it a passing figure of speech soon dated, already has had its heyday?
Most likely my curiosity about the phrase will eventually just die down.

Maybe what it means depends on a shrug, raised eyebrow, tone, or frown.
There's something about the saying that's mysterious, illusive, unique—
most likely my curiosity about the phrase will eventually just die down.
"It is what it is" a clerk replied to my comment how busy she was last week.

J.C. Penney Litany

The men's section soothing and solid, offering after offering of shirts on armless plastic, necks neatly chopped

Flannel, Poplin, Wool, Cotton, Chambray, Chamois, Corduroy, Micro-suede

A mother toting child and diaper bag, another with stroller and United States flag

A passing procession of Pierre Cardin made in Korea, Stafford made in Guatemala, St. John's Bay made in Bangladesh, Van Heusen made in Thailand

Amber, Indigo, Basil, Blue Abyss, Oatmeal, Olive, Espresso, Mushroom

Pale light from high windows reveals not a man in sight

A Hardcover Book

Carrying a hardcover book and not that popular electronic tool
I get polite, benevolent smiles seemingly reserved for the old;
people ask, "How old's your Bible?" as if I'd broken some rule.

I'm asked it so often I'm disappointed when I'm not—you'll
find it easy to believe it could be true in any size household—
Carrying a hardcover book and not that popular electronic tool

even admitting the chances low of it happening when polled.
Please be assured I'm still thinking straight, am OK, all told;
people ask, "How old's your Bible?" as if I'd broken some rule;

they learned most likely long ago while going to grade school
how to be very comfortable, complacent, following the fold.
Carrying a hardcover book and not that popular electronic tool

is not quite correct and some may frown, see you the fool,
quite the dinosaur, out of touch—even sprinkled with mold:
people ask, "How old's your Bible?" as if I'd broken some rule

that one should flow with the crowd—not intending to be cruel.
But I'll continue to read instead of text and not be controlled:
Carrying a hardcover book and not that popular electronic tool
people ask, "How old's your Bible?" as if I'd broken some rule.

You Know

its Truth when it's
simple, elegant,
somehow familiar—
leaving you washed
in disbelief you never
saw it before.

The Rub

Dreams—tectonic plates of our
subconscious without our choosing,
reminds us of those famous lines:
"To sleep—perchance to dream:
ay, there's the rub."

The Line

Today the fast food place line was extra long—
customers waiting like in a church confession
obtaining support by being one of the throng
in line with other fellow souls in procession.

Customers waiting like in a church confession
contemplating photos of shakes, fries, and cones
in line with other fellow souls in procession
rationalizing one day they'll just be bones—

contemplating photos of shakes, fries, and cones,
pushing aside New Year Resolutions not long ago
rationalizing one day they'll just be bones
thinking eating healthy is a tough row to hoe.

Pushing aside New Year Resolutions not long ago
ignoring cholesterol, sugar, starch, and fat
thinking eating healthy is a tough row to hoe
instead believe themselves with stomach flat

ignoring cholesterol, sugar, starch, and fat,
staring at the wall menu with caloric red flags
instead believe themselves with stomach flat
disregarding additions to saddle bags.

Staring at the wall menu with caloric red flags
obtaining support by being one of the throng
disregarding additions to saddle bags—
today the fast food place line was extra long.

III.
The Domestic

A Supermarket Triptych

Did the passersby think I was a restaurant owner instead of there
to enjoy the colossal bags and jars Alice in Wonderland size?
A Motown tune belted out love and emotions—places I didn't dare.
Did the passersby think I was a restaurant owner instead of there
to wonder, check the sales, notice anything new, leisurely stare
as I sip my courtesy cup of decaf, speculate on good looking guys?
Did the passersby think I was a restaurant owner instead of there
to enjoy the colossal bags and jars Alice in Wonderland size?

The middle of supermarket aisles are good as neither side receives
any preference as if Queen Elizabeth surveying waiting fans,
nodding to the Clabber Girl while sipping decaf, A.M. Reprieve.
The middle of supermarket aisles are good as neither side receives
a longer inspection than the other especially when one perceives
potato chips, chocolate on sale—best run to the aisle of pans.
The middle of supermarket aisles are good as neither side receives
any preference as if Queen Elizabeth surveying waiting fans.

The grocery bottles of extra virgin oil stood in extra straight lines
on top shelves, labels maroon or yellow—the white delightfully prim
covering their round fronts facing aisles as if fashion runway designs.
The grocery bottles of extra virgin oil stood in extra straight lines
exotic, sophisticated, as if competing with bottles of imported wines
so not to be neglected, sidelined—relegated to bottom shelf confines.
The grocery bottles of extra virgin oil stood in extra straight lines
on top shelves, labels maroon or yellow—the white delightfully prim.

Hanging Clothes on Clotheslines

Save energy instead of using dryers like you're used to—
before using lines wipe with a clean damp cloth each time,
hang sheets so they block clothes you prefer others not to view.

Wash on the traditional Monday and don't be afraid of the dew:
no matter your age, if you work fulltime, or aren't in your prime—
save energy instead of using dryers like you're used to.

Pin up shirts by their tails, pants by cuffs, even if doing a few
and it is best to hang them so they're quite dry by dinnertime;
hang sheets so they block clothes you prefer others not to see.

Be neat and remove clothes pins to avoid them gathering grime,
and it's fine to use one pin instead of two if you only have a few.
Save energy instead of using dryers like you're used to.

Pin up socks by the toe; keep hanging clothes—follow through
as they stand straight when harvesting frozen in wintertime:
hang sheets so they block clothes you prefer others not to view.

Do try this advice as you'll find it is solid, tested, and quite true
and you'll find taking clothes down also a relaxing pastime.
Save energy instead of using dryers like you're used to—
hang sheets so they block clothes you prefer others not to view.

The Car Wash

Attendants stopped towel snapping
to smile at a strange woman driver
ignoring the most snow of the season.

Green hula girl plastic strips rotated
warm water streams each side the
long, empty, fogged car wash tunnel.

As the door opened, a muffled eared
boy banished me from misty tropics
to make solitary tracks in white.

Sewing by Day

A chair by a window is best for selecting pieces in quilt making:
light of day, natural light, best reveals shades, flaws in pieces
of boxes on boxes of clothes carefully cut—a slow undertaking;
quilt after quilt has made my children question output increases.

Light of day, natural light, best reveals shades, flaws in pieces.
"Who's your quilts for?" I'm asked as stacked quilts grow higher.
Quilt after quilt has made my children question output increases
and I picture the stacks after I'm gone going up in a night pyre.

"Who's your quilts for?" I'm asked as stacked quilts grow higher:
plaid, plain, striped, flowered, flannel, fleece, denim, cotton
and I picture the stacks after I'm gone going up in a night pyre—
memories stored in cut clothes and pieces not yet forgotten.

Plaid, plain, striped, flowered, flannel, fleece, denim, cotton
of boxes on boxes of clothes carefully cut—a slow undertaking:
memories stored in cut clothes and pieces not yet forgotten.
A chair by a window is best for selecting pieces in quilt making.

The Sewing Box

Button Bottle

Glass, with a metal cap, a
hair-wax dressing bottle for crew,
burr haircuts from a garage
sale too good to let go.

It was now half full (or half empty)
a changing gyroscope of snaps,
safety pins, screws, buttons buffered
by orphan thread.

Thread Bag

A myriad of spools, a bird's nest of
tangled thread: a 15Ë wooden spool of
dusty rose spilled out and another still
unused with a bump hinting thread
hidden by its label.

Needle Assortment

Curved, beading, packing, sailmakers,
carpet, secured in a cardboard packet—
a gift for joining the American Handcraft
Club. Made in Redditch, England all shiny
and still used for rag rugs, tying quilts.

Tray

The tray came with the latched box my
husband gave me and held: thread, needles,
safety pins, thimble, embroidery thread, scissors,
hooks and eyes, string. A ribboned hat pin holder,
potholder loops, a bread wrapper tie, tape measure,
a mending kit from the Hyatt.

Back Pocket

Iron on patches, elastic, heart sachet, denim for a doll
never finished for my daughter, decorative braid from
a ski jacket, hem cutter, folded white store lace and eyelet;
yarn from my cousin with skeins labeled BELA, BLACKIE,
the sheep shorn for it. Another mending kit from the Hyatt.

Crochet in the Round

A ring of white crocheted pineapples that'd outlived the
pillow case it was once married. When alone again, I sewed
it on a new J.C. Penney's case with extra strong thread to
clutch on sleepless nights.

A Needle Holder

Two layers of thick felt, a lighter weight of green sandwiched
like lettuce from a great-aunt sheltering a long pearl hat pin,
two tarnished needles, and a straight pin akimbo.

Soap Holder

The crocheted holder turtle shaped, with a bar of soap made
by my grandmother who said when you sew you were not lonely—
the one who made bibs for grandfather's calendar girls
in the bathroom.

The Last Doll

She's the last doll I got for Christmas, the only one with long hair
and she sits with two other survivors grouped in conversation
in a pink dress with three shiny buttons without compare.

She has puffed sleeves, white shoes and stockings to wear
and a new place within the group in steady rotation;
she's the last doll I got for Christmas, the only one with long hair.

The doll has no name as she seemed so rare
with braided long hair that deserved much admiration
in a pink dress with three shiny buttons without compare.

Sitting with the others she rules over them with flare,
her arms extended as if receiving ovations;
she's the last doll I got for Christmas, the only one with long hair.

Still looking new, she has needed no repair
and sits very erect as fitting her station
in a pink dress with three shiny buttons without compare.

But of the survivors, she's the one I could spare
because she's not been held as often for validation;
she's the last doll I got for Christmas, the only one with long hair
in a pink dress with three shiny buttons without compare.

A Dishwashing Liquid Pantoum

There are so many on the shelves but had to select one—
antibacterial, concentrated, degreaser, biodegradable:
how bad were phosphates (what did they do) in the long run?
Surely an experienced housekeeper should be capable.

Antibacterial, concentrated, degreaser, biodegradable—
what's anionic surfactants, PPG-26, sodium laueth sulfate?
Surely an experienced housekeeper should be capable.
Could early soap made from ashes be just as great?

What's anionic surfactants, PPG-26, sodium laueth sulfate?
How could someone who's read all her life not know—
could early soap made from ashes be just as great?
That stock boy probably thinks I'm lost from some chateau.

How could someone who's read all her life not know
which aren't tested on animals, are good for the ecosystem?
That stock boy probably thinks I'm lost from some chateau
ignorant of what's proven safe for a home septic system.

Which aren't tested on animals, are good for the ecosystem?
I was looking at illustrations of orange owls and blue rain
ignorant of what's proven safe for a home septic system
as I checked if the color of lemons on labels was the same.

I was looking at illustrations of orange owls and blue rain
when a man came, looked a second, walked away with one
as I checked if the color of lemons on labels was the same
studying price per ounce, if degreasing power was overdone

when a man came, looked a second, walked away with one.
It was time to stop wondering about ULTRA, comparing scents,
studying price per ounce, if degreasing power was overdone,
looking for warnings, and which ones saved a few cents.

It was time to stop wondering about ULTRA, comparing scents,
how bad were phosphates (what did they do) in the long run,
looking for warnings, and which ones saved a few cents:
there are so many on the shelves but had to select one.

The Key

to my p.o. box is still shiny obtained after
contents of my rural box kept getting
scattered down the road
like garments in a steamy film.

Shopping at Tom's

Tears filled her eyes imagining her funeral
procession extending to the dairy counter.
Aisle 4 featured stacked boxes of fortune cookies—
removing just one bottom box would bring them
crashing; she smiled as she ducked under
a banner of chickens in yellow straw hats

followed by turkeys in hiking boots. After a
hysterectomy did they package your remains in a
paper sack like the gizzard, heart, liver, neck,
inside a roasting chicken? Chives, cilantro leaves,
cinnamon. It was good to see the Morton Salt girl
under her umbrella still pouring salt. She'd used

saltboxes with the top and bottom removed to hold
gifts for the kids at Christmas. When she was
walking past the peanuts she remembered buying
small gifts. She went to see if the SunMaid girl
in her red bonnet with long ties was still
effortlessly holding that huge tray of green grapes.

She recalled the restaurant next door, listening to
old men talk about how rabbits made runways in the
woods, about walking in circles in the snow. The
steam rose from the coffee maker by the men sitting
closely shoulder to shoulder, saw again the holes
in their shoes, holes that gave them personality.

The men were always the same men on the same stools.
Next time she'd check the labels of Clabber Girl Baking
Powder: the girl carrying the plate of perfectly tall,
uniform, stacked golden brown biscuits was always
there with a Mona Lisa smile—but was she walking
to put them on the table or on the way to eat them?

The sitting woman on the label seemed to be sewing but
could be plucking a goose, it was hard to see clearly.
One of the tabloids read: *Moses Spotted Walking
on Miami Beach*. Had other women felt failures when
their biscuits never matched those on the label,
used a magnifying glass to see the sitting woman?

Shallow Boxes

Quilting pieces, stacked in shallow cardboard boxes from a grocery store
to be ready when sleep eludes, each box with choices of cut up clothes—
protection like the Maginot Line against invasions of bad dreams, a war
fought by women with a needle to seem next day fresh as a primrose.

To be ready when sleep eludes, each box with choices of cut up clothes,
sandbag sewing scraps of twill, denim, wool, fleece, flannel, cotton:
fought by women with a needle to seem next day fresh as a primrose
after giving up tossing and turning—the past a jumble not forgotten.

Sandbag sewing scraps of twill, denim, wool, fleece, flannel, cotton:
protection like the Maginot Line against invasions of bad dreams, a war
after giving up tossing and turning—the past a jumble not forgotten:
quilting pieces, stacked in shallow cardboard boxes from a grocery store.

Arranging Spices on Your Shelf

By color—Basil, Chives, Parsley, Thyme:
Onion can be salt, granulated, minced.
An alphabetical list can be very long—big time
and I'm not sure many would be convinced.

Onion can be salt, granulated, minced:
Pepper: Cayenne, Seasoned, Black:
and I'm not sure many would be convinced
if rubs were included—there could be flack.

Pepper: Cayenne, Seasoned, Black;
by seed: Caraway, Celery, Dill:
if rubs were included there could be flack,
an arrangement questionable to fit the bill.

By seed: Caraway, Celery, Dill:
Leaves: Bay, Rosemary, Thyme
an arrangement questionable to fit the bill—
by now you've had enough of rhyme.

Leaves: Bay, Rosemary, Thyme
an alphabetical list can be very long—big time,
by now you've had enough of rhyme:
by color—Basil, Chives, Parsley, Thyme.

Shades of Gray

Dawn arrived through tightly closed blinds: the room getting
form where the ceiling ended and wall began with different
shades of gray—the chair against the window acquiring shape.
The vertical spindles on the bed were becoming visible—
there was no mistaking another day without sleep.

Perhaps it would be good to make very hot tea or coffee, end
the limbo. The lace added to the top sheet becomes important
to grasp and you're grateful to have a pen in your other hand—
but wonder how much you'll be able to read. Earplugs keep
it a silent film and you smile picturing Charlie Chaplin.

Capturing the Moon

through Venetian blinds
is a matter of
adjusting the pull,
your eyes—and timing.

IV.
Speculations

Prufrock Napkins

The white 2-fold napkins dispense like tongues at Burger King
Subway's are handkerchief square with printing in lettuce green
McDonalds's 4-folds, embossed M's fluttering like doves on wing
Taco Bell's 3-folds the color of refried beans
Wendy's white 3-fold with pig-tailed girl, completes the scene.

Deciding on how to fold as with damask for a napkin ring,
surveying food on plastic trays as haute cuisine
are daily events making one upswing.
He smoothes paper napkins assuming them ironed things:
how could a wrinkle presume, what could that mean?

Wiping yellow fog from windows transforms napkins to string
and he drives home reinforced by caffeine
remembering rooms the women come and go
talking of Michelangelo
wondering if he's been seen.

A Matter of Location

1

Because it has no outlet,
the Dead Sea, the deepest
crack on earth is ten times
saltier than any ocean—
one glass can kill you

Between Israel and Jordan,
is where two continental
plates continue to tear
apart

2

Line upon line
spun off easily in dreams
that on waking,
turned into balls:
bouncing off reason
they tangled

3

That inner point is our
center they say—but not yet,
not yet—the fear of finding
nothing is still too strong

Near the Library Window

I reread the words about
mythology becoming obsolete if
man only applied his reason.

The fog outside seemed to rub
Prufrock's question,
"What is it?" It must've known
napping students were not
talking of Michelangelo.

It started to rain but turned
to snow and melted on the
landing.

Why Does the Moon Shine?

I glimpsed the Moon through closed blinds last night
and figured with so much light it must be in full phase
but why did it shine in the first place, give such light?

Trying to understand, science facts didn't seem right:
rotations, orbits, math, and logic appeared but haze—
I glimpsed the moon through closed blinds last night.

Yes, the Moon orbits the Earth—both also in flight
circling the Sun...it was late and I felt more in a daze:
but why did it shine in the first place, give such light?

Defining moon, star planet became blurry, less outright
and in the dark couldn't help but wonder and gaze:
I glimpsed the Moon through closed blinds last night.

Does Earth shine in space if clouds are out of sight?
Is there a Woman in the Moon—the side without rays?
I glimpsed the Moon through closed blinds last night
but why did it shine in the first place, give such light?

Catching On

Only I think everything's talked out too much.
It's talked out so much that it's not felt.
                    John Galsworthy

Do we really accept what
Copernicus said about the
Earth not being the center
of things?

We're still figuring out
what to do with Darwin—
and women's equality.

The Radio Said

three soldiers had been uncovered,
frozen since World War 1 in the Alps,
leather belts, stars on their caps,
gas masks intact.

I didn't catch which side they were on,
but perhaps they weren't American
because my uncle had no star on his
wide brimmed hat, his coat had no belt.
He came back from the trenches with
shell shock pursuing him till he died.

A Matter of Lines

1

It's a toss up which postal
clerk you get: the one always
smiling or the frowning one
you think more sincere

Both have the tone of
priests in confessionals
murmuring, "What's inside?"

When finished, you pretend not
to see the others waiting,
departing with downcast eyes

2

Corn the color of worn
gold in straight lines
molded by prevailing wind,
graceful before the fall

3

Line upon line spun off
easily in dreams:
on waking they
turned into balls—
bouncing off reason
they tangled

Examples

of women with bound feet are still around in China:
the painful binding done by mothers when girls are
about five to make them look better, prepare them
for good marriages.

Western women congratulate themselves they do
not follow such things—but what about Cinderella
fitting the small slipper, the stiletto heels surely to
attract the prince.

Last Night

sheets were taunt sails
flaying the Moon, and
Rings of Saturn,
till being snagged
by Dawn became
cocooned

In Kansas

The Greeks had many gods to blame their
misfortune: we can only conclude God is
absent, doesn't care, or is doing it for
our own good.

I sought Dorothy's reassurance without
the wish to be in Kansas; maybe I hadn't
chanted, "There's no place like home"
enough—then too, I hadn't her red shoes.

There Were Only

a few lights on in the library, no car tracks in the parking lot,
a gentle rain reinforcing the nose as the most elemental of
the senses. It was a much-needed rain that could be too late
for crops—a neighbor saying corn ears were very small.
So much rain early spring and then the lushness turned brittle brown.

Maybe there weren't any car tracks in the parking lot because
of the rain but when I reached the library, a couple said it was
closed. It was sad to think of computers blinking in the empty
library like solitary lighthouses.

I lift my face to capture the rain of childhood and failing,
remember the earth is covered mostly with water and we know
less about oceans then the moon—and wonder how much
wonder is lost in knowing.

Salt on Fast Food Trays

Size and placement random, salt's usually unnoticed on empty trays.
After placemat's are shaken—one can connect the grains
and make endless nebulas, constellations, clusters on lucky days
concluding star watchers not living in cities have many gains.

After placemat's are shaken, one can connect the grains—
remember what our ancestors did from the beginning of time
concluding star watchers not living in cities have many gains,
making one want to travel, explore: it looks not that far to climb.

Remember what our ancestors did from the beginning of time:
leaving us names what they saw—we still know Pleiades—
making one want to travel, explore: it looks not that far to climb:
join the daughters of Atlas fleeing from Orion would be a breeze.

Leaving us names what they saw, we still know Pleiades;
we can see the fiery Swan Nebula where stars are born
join the daughters of Atlas fleeing from Orion would be a breeze:
the images we see makes everything else appear shopworn.

We can see the fiery Swan Nebula where stars are born
and make endless nebulas, constellations, clusters on lucky days—
the images we see makes everything else appear shopworn:
size and placement random, salt's usually unnoticed on empty trays.

A Room of My Own

A skeleton slumps in the
waiting room chair wearing
a sign: "So, think you've
been waitin' long?"

My name called, I get a
room of my own with an
enlargement of a heart,
and read my weight fits
one three inches taller.

Select Moments

There was a time not long ago
Striving to feel the Earth turn
I spread like a child making
Snow angels on summer grass:
Couldn't one see clouds move?

I strained to detect movement
Like a forked divining rod
Searching for water despite
Reason saying it would be
Impossible even if rotating
Thousands of miles an hour
and circling the Sun.

Further back in years, I stared
A long time at a particular spot
One night at stars that appeared
Extra close waiting for any
Clues what it was all about.

Surely if I stood tall as possible
Long enough, tried hard enough
there'd come hints, some pattern?

The Reading Room

offers shelf after shelf of magazines slanting conveniently,
row after row of newspapers labels
like white aprons on neat housewives.

Club upholstered chairs, tables with marble tops
as Victorian as a men's reading room clustered
in conversation groups.

I lift the wooden spindle holding
The New York Review of Books where annotations
are divided into Humanities or Science.

Sleeping Beauty

was awakened by the prince.
What would've happened if
she hadn't been a beauty?

Epilogue

Patterns

The sky today was cumulus clouds:
the choice too immense, I chose one
to secure the secret of time and space,
forget spinning on a planet.

Author Biography

Carol Smallwood's over five dozen books includes: *Women on Poetry: Writing, Revising, Publishing and Teaching*, noted on *Poets & Writers Magazine* list of Best Books for Writers. Recent anthologies include: *Writing After Retirement: Tips by Successful Retired Writers* (Rowman & Littlefield, 2014); *Bringing the Arts into the Library: An Outreach Handbook* (American Library Association, 2014); *Library Partnerships with Writers and Poets: Case Studies* (McFarland, 2017).

Recent literary collections include: *Water, Earth, Air, Fire, and Picket Fences* (Lamar University Press, 2014); *Divining the Prime Meridian* (WordTech Editions, 2015); *Interweavings: Creative Nonfiction* (Shanti Arts, 2017); *In Hubble's Shadow* (Shanti Arts, 2017); *Prisms, Particles, and Refractions* (Finishing Line Press, 2017). *Prisms, Particles, and Refractions* was nominated for the Society of Midland Authors Award in Poetry.

Carol has founded and supports humane societies. She's received multiple Pushcart Prize nominations and appears in *Who's Who in America; Who's Who in the World.*